To Isla
For being good.
MERRY CHRISTMAS!
From Aunty Ann & Uncle Bob.
xox

Each and every Christmas Eve's Eve (the day before Christmas Eve), Santa checked his list to see which boy or girl had been extra good. Whoever was at the top of the list would be invited to meet all the reindeer, elves and of course Santa himself.

At the very top of his list was...

...ISLA

Rudolph (the fastest of all the reindeer) flew straight to her house and popped her on his back.

Then quick as a flash they zoomed back to see everyone.

She had a fantastic day, helping the elves prepare the presents for all the good boys and girls.

Early on Christmas Eve morning, Santa was about to get dressed when he noticed something was wrong!

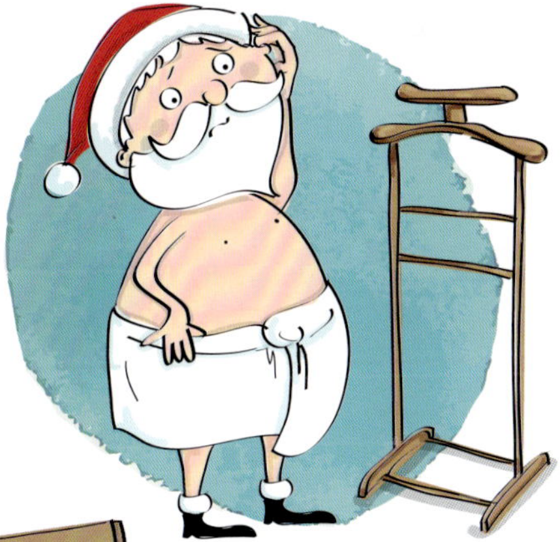

His bright red suit was GONE!

Santa looked in his wardrobe but it wasn't there.

Then he looked on the back of his door.

He even looked under his bed but his suit was nowhere to be found!

"Oh no, this is terrible!" exclaimed Santa. "I can't deliver Christmas presents without my suit on!"

A very red-faced and worried Santa called for Isla and the elves to come into the grotto's great hall to tell them the awful news that his suit was missing.

Santa then asked all his little helpers to try and find the suit or he would have to cancel Christmas!

Santa didn't want
to cancel Christmas.

So he tried on a
green elf suit
but it was
too small.

Then he tried on
Mrs Claus's dress
But it was too short.

Finally, he tried on
Rudolph's very best blanket...
but it was too big,
too itchy and very smelly!

Santa didn't know what to do.

Isla and the elves looked all over Santa's Grotto. They looked in the toy-making room.

They looked in the kitchen.

They looked in the present-wrapping room.

They looked in Santa's workshop.

They even looked in the reindeer's stinky stables.

But Santa's suit was nowhere to be found.

Isla noticed two tiny elves.
They were hiding something behind their backs.

Isla said hello, to the elves.
"What are you hiding behind your backs?"

The sorry-looking elves showed Isla what they were hiding. It was Santa's bright red suit but it was as tiny as a baby's bib!

The elves explained to Isla that they had been trying to help Santa by washing his suit but it had shrunk! Now they didn't know what to do.

Suddenly Isla had a FANTASTIC idea!

Isla asked the two elves to go and look for:

Some white tinsel.

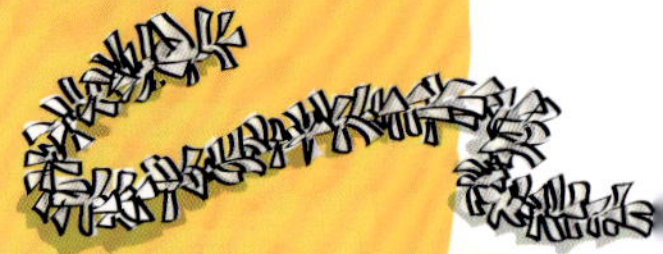

Some black ribbon.
Some shiny gold paper...

...and three big, round decorations.

Then bring them to Santa's workshop as quickly as possible.

The elves found everything on the list and placed each one on the workshop table.

"Perfect!" said Isla
as she pulled out a huge piece of red material and put it on the table.
"We're going to make Santa
a brand new suit," she said.

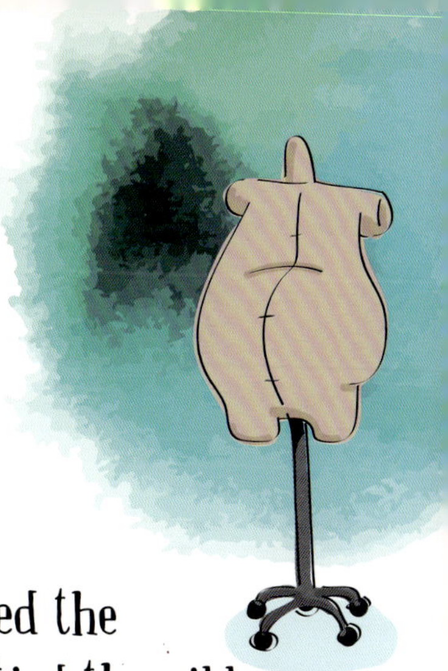

They glued the tinsel, tied the ribbon and cut out the shiny gold paper.

Then they sewed on the bright decorations.

Finally it was all finished...
but had they made it in time?

A very nervous Santa looked at the **big** cuckoo clock on the wall.

It would soon be too late to start delivering the presents.

Santa was going to have to cancel Christmas!

Just as he was telling the reindeer the bad news that they might not be flying this year...

Santa was taken aback as Isla and her two helpers ran into the room with his brand new, bright red suit.

It had a tinsel collar and cuffs.

A belt and buckle made of shiny gold paper...

...and three beautiful decorations as buttons.

Santa was very surprised
and extremely happy.

He tried on his new suit.

It was PERFECT!

HO HO HO!

Santa was
smiling again.

And so were
all the elves,
reindeer and Mrs Claus
- because Christmas
was back on!

"Thank you so much, you have saved Christmas!" exclaimed Santa, as he climbed into his sleigh to head off to deliver all the presents. "But where did you find the red fabric?"

Isla just smiled as she got ready to make her way home.

"EEEK!" cried Mrs Claus.
"WHO cut this giant
hole in my curtains?!"

The end